RAPTORS

HAWKS

JULIE K. LUNDGREN

ROURKE PUBLISHING

Vero Beach, Florida 32964

www.rourkepublishing.com

Project Assistance:
The author also thanks raptor specialist Frank Taylor and the team at Blue Door Publishing.

Photo credits: Cover © Risan; Title Page © Brooke Whatnall; Contents Page © anotherlook; Page 4 © F Taylor; Page 5 © Leisa Hennessy; Page 6 © Alan Merrigan; Page 7 © F Taylor; Page 8 © Dan Cardiff; Page 9 © Jill Lang; Page 10 © Gregg Williams; Page 11 © Michael Stubblefield; Page 12 © J.T. Lewis; Page 12b - George Allen Penton; Page 13 © F Taylor; Page 14 © Thomas O'Neil; Page 15 © Cornelius Fischer; Page 17 © B.G. Smith; Page 18 © Michael Fritzen; Page 19 © Joseph Gareri; Page 21 © Eric McDonald; Page 22 © Dan Cardiff

Editor: Meg Greve

Cover and page design by Nicola Stratford, Blue Door Publishing

Library of Congress Cataloging-in-Publication Data

Lundgren, Julie K.
  Hawks / Julie K. Lundgren.
      p. cm. -- (Raptors)
      Includes index.
  ISBN 978-1-60694-397-7 (hard cover)
  ISBN 978-1-60694-775-3 (soft cover)
1. Hawks--Juvenile literature. I. Title.
QL696.F32L864 2010
  598.9'44--dc22

                                      2009000530

Rourke Publishing
Printed in the United States of America, North Mankato, Minnesota
081810
081710LP-B

www.rourkepublishing.com - rourke@rourkepublishing.com
Post Office Box 643328 Vero Beach, Florida 32964

Contents

Sky Riders

Raptors, or birds of **prey**, catch and eat other animals. Hawks are raptors. They live all over the world. People who study birds divide hawks into three groups called **accipiters**, **buteos**, and **harriers**. Like most raptors, hawk females outweigh males.

Adult sharp-shinned hawks, a kind of small accipiter, have red eyes.

4

Accipiters have short, rounded wings and long tails. They live in forests.

5

Red-tailed hawks
and other buteos
soar on the wind.
The long feathers
at their wingtips and in
their tails help them steer.

6

Buteos have broad wings and soar over more open country. They live in grasslands, cropland, places that have a mixture of woods and clearings, and even deserts. Red-tailed hawks, one kind of buteo, often perch on fence posts or telephone poles next to roadsides and fields.

Harriers have narrow wings, long tails, and faces like owls. They prefer to live near grasslands, meadows, or marshes.

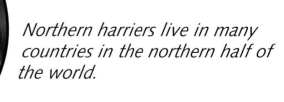

Northern harriers live in many countries in the northern half of the world.

BUILT TO KILL

Hawk bodies have special tools that make them expert hunters. Hawks slice and tear meat with their sharp, hooked beaks. Like human fingernails, raptor beaks wear down and grow back over time.

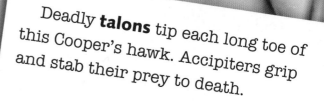

Deadly **talons** tip each long toe of this Cooper's hawk. Accipiters grip and stab their prey to death.

RAPTOR REPORT

IMPORTANT

IMPORTANT

Short, rounded wings allow Cooper's hawks to avoid branches while flying after prey in the woods.

Harriers fly low in search of rodents, birds, insects, and dead animals. The ruff of feathers around their faces captures sound, allowing them to locate hidden prey. Owls, another kind of raptor, have this feature, too.

While most hawks hunt alone, Harris's hawks hunt in groups of two to five. They live in the dry lands of Mexico and the southwestern United States. They hunt rabbits, rodents, snakes, and birds.

Harris's hawks use teamwork to capture prey. They take turns scaring prey out of hiding for the others to chase down.

Northern harrier males have gray feathers with black wingtips. Females have brown feathers.

Red-tails and other hawks can have individual color differences.

Hawks and other raptors depend on their sharp eyes to hunt. They have a special extra pair of eyelids for protection. It keeps their eyes moist and sweeps away dust while still allowing them to see.

The special eyelid sweeps from one corner of this red-tailed hawk's eye to the other. The hawk can see through this layer.

FAMILY TIME

Most buteos and accipiters build stick nests in trees. Harriers usually make grassy nests on the ground. Both parents take care of the eggs. After about a month, the eggs hatch. Downy feathers help keep the young warm.

Red-tailed hawk nestlings learn to fly, or fledge, about six weeks after hatching.

This Harris's hawk youngster has begun growing its flight feathers.

Masterful Migrators

Because prey is harder to find during winter, many hawks migrate each fall from their summer nesting grounds to warmer areas. Some travel across entire continents.

Swainson's hawks migrate thousands of miles in the fall from North America to Argentina. They return to North America in the spring.

Swainson's hawks take about two months to complete their migration one way.

Unlike geese and ducks, hawks do not migrate by constantly flapping their wings. Instead they allow columns of rising warm air, called thermals, to lift them. They soar to great heights, and then glide away to find the next thermal.

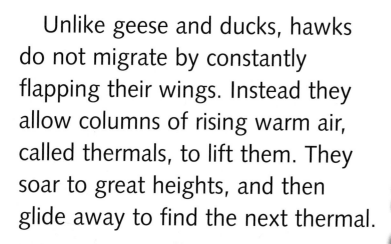

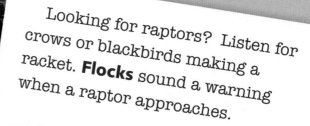

Looking for raptors? Listen for crows or blackbirds making a racket. **Flocks** sound a warning when a raptor approaches.

RAPTOR REPORT

Like many migrating birds, rough-legged hawks migrate in groups. They travel from arctic areas south to parts of the United States, Europe, and Asia.

Helpful Hawks

Throughout time, people and **predators** have fought to get along with each other. People shoot hawks, fearing they will kill their animals. Almost all hawks prefer wild prey. They help keep pest populations down. Raptors can carry only a fraction of their body weight, so pets everywhere remain safe.

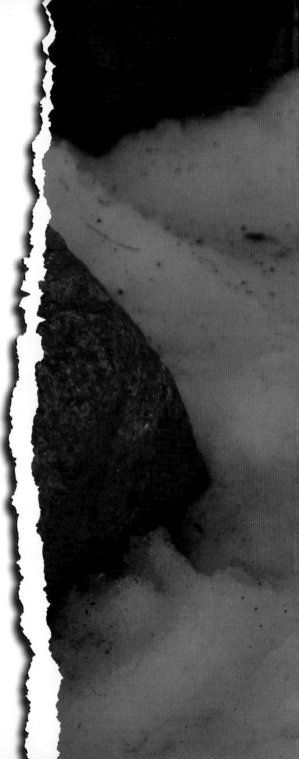

Raptors with injuries that do not heal properly sometimes go to live at zoos and raptor centers. A caretaker has fed this broad-winged hawk a mouse.

Get to know raptors in your area. Take a walk with someone who knows about birds. Check out a nature center or zoo to see them up close. Keep your eyes on the skies for fierce, handsome hawks!

GLOSSARY

accipiters (ack-SIP-uh-terz): forest hawks with short, rounded wings and long tails, like Cooper's hawks and sharp-shinned hawks

buteos (BOO-tee-ohz): hawks with long, broad wings for soaring, like red-tailed hawks and broad-winged hawks

flocks (FLOKS): a group of one kind of bird

harriers (HAIR-ee-yerz): birds of prey with slim bodies and long, narrow wings, who usually fly low to the ground, like northern harriers and spotted harriers

migrate (MYE-grate): to move from one area to another according to the seasons

predators (PRED-uh-turs): animals that hunt other animals

prey (PRAY): animals that are hunted and eaten by other animals

talons (TAL-uhnz): a raptor's sharp claws

Index

Websites to Visit

Soar over to your local library to learn more about hawks and other raptors. Hunt down the following websites:

www.birds.cornell.edu
www.biologicaldiversity.org/index.html
www.hawkandowl.org
www.hawkmountain.org
www.hawkridge.org

About The Author

Julie K. Lundgren grew up near Lake Superior where she reveled in mucking about in the woods, picking berries, and expanding her rock collection. Her interest in nature led her to a degree in biology and eight years of volunteer work at The Raptor Center at the University of Minnesota. She currently lives in Minnesota with her husband and two sons.